Coping Skills

Tools & Techniques For Every Stressful Situation

FAITH G. HARPER,
PhD, LPC-S, ACS, ACN

MICROCOSM PUBLISHING
Portland, Ore

COPING SKILLS
Tools & Techniques for Every Stressful Situation

Part of the 5 Minute Therapy Series
© Dr. Faith Harper, 2016, 2019
This edition © Microcosm Publishing, 2019
First edition, first published 2016
Second edition, first published June 11, 2019
Second printing, 3000 copies, July 2020

ISBN 978-1-62106-139-7
This is Microcosm #280
Book design and infographics by Joe Biel

For a catalog, write or visit:
Microcosm Publishing
2752 N Williams Ave.
Portland, OR 97227
www.Microcosm.Pub

To join the ranks of high-class stores that feature Microcosm titles, talk to your rep: In the U.S. **Como** (Atlantic), **Fujii** (Midwest), **Book Travelers West** (Pacific), **Turnaround** in Europe, **Manda/UTP** in Canada, **New South** in Australia, and **GPS** in Asia, India, Africa, and South America. We are sold in the gift market by **Gifts of Nature.**

If you bought this on Amazon, I'm so sorry because you could have gotten it cheaper and supported a small, independent publisher at **Microcosm.Pub**

Global labor conditions are bad, and our roots in industrial Cleveland in the 70s and 80s made us appreciate the need to treat workers right. Therefore, our books are MADE IN THE USA and printed on post-consumer paper.

Library of Congress Cataloging-in-Publication Data
Names: Harper, Faith G., author.
Title: Coping skills : tools & techniques for every stressful situation /
    Faith G. Harper, PhD, LPC-S, ACS, ACN.
Description: Portland, Oregon : Microcosm Publishing, [2019] | Series: 5
    minute therapy | Includes bibliographical references.
Identifiers: LCCN 2018039080 | ISBN 9781621061397 (pbk.)
Subjects: LCSH: Self-help techniques. | Stress management.
Classification: LCC BF632 .H266 2019 | DDC 158.1--dc23
LC record available at https://lccn.loc.gov/2018039080

MICROCOSM · PUBLISHING

Microcosm Publishing is Portland's most diversified publishing house and distributor with a focus on the colorful, authentic, and empowering. Our books and zines have put your power in your hands since 1996, equipping readers to make positive changes in their lives and in the world around them. Microcosm emphasizes skill-building, showing hidden histories, and fostering creativity through challenging conventional publishing wisdom with books and bookettes about DIY skills, food, bicycling, gender, self-care, and social justice. What was once a distro and record label was started by Joe Biel in his bedroom and has become among the oldest independent publishing houses in Portland, OR. We are a politically moderate, centrist publisher in a world that has inched to the right for the past 80 years.

Contents

Introduction: Shit's Fucked

We are all cursed with living in interesting times. Even when shit is rocking along and our lives are generally positive, we are not fucking likely to focus on calmness or give ourselves space to think and chill. Remember when vacations were meant to be a time to have fun adventures? Now it's a time to go away and sit somewhere and be as quiet, non-thinky, and non-doey as possible. I work with so many people who just need more time in their lives to chill. They aren't crazy, they are just fucking *exhausted*.

We are all seeking better ways to live with all this shit, right? When I say "all this shit" I am talking about what it means to be human in the 21st century. We are living in a time of huge uncertainty. Political upheaval, community violence, environmental distress. We are hyper-wired and overstimulated. And undernourished in all the ways that matter: authentic connection, stillness, healthy nourishment, joyful movement. We are seeking relief even more desperately than Aidan Quinn was seeking Susan.

Let's look at what's gotten super popular in recent years. Pokemon Go. Fidget spinners. Coloring. My older (and therefore more middle aged than I am) brother succumbed to the planking craze a few years ago. These are all things that help soothe our minds when life is a dumpster fire. And there will likely be at least three more viral coping skill activities sweeping Insta between now and when this book is published. We *need* shit to help manage life stress. These are all *coping skills activities*. We are all actively seeking ways to manage things that feel unmanageable.

So before we talk about specific types of coping skills and how they work and all that therapist-y bullshit, I want to say a few things as clearly as possible and as *loudly* as possible for those of y'all hovering around in the back.

Needing coping skills is not a sign of weakness or mental illness. It means you are a normal human being navigating a truly abnormal culture. Lily Tomlin once said, *"Reality is the leading cause of stress amongst those in touch with it."*

There are a few things that are complete and fundamental truths about yourself and why you sometimes are struggling and need coping skills:

- There are no such things as wrong responses, only adaptive ones.

- What you have survived has wired your body to proceed with extreme caution, on an unconscious level at all times. This is called staying fucking alive and safe.

- You are not choosing to shut down.

- This is not a "mental" illness; it is a physiological state of the human body.

- You are not crazy; you have adapted to the environment around you with the only information you had at the time…your previous circumstances.

You may be thinking, *"Bitch, stop being overly nice and letting me off the hook. I'm just fucking crazy and I don't need an apologist right now."*

Yeah, here's the thing. I'm not nice. Empathic? Definitely. But nice and letting people off the hook? Never been accused of that in the history of ever. You are absolutely accountable for your actions, no matter what bullshit has been foisted upon you. You may not have been the one who bought the ticket, but it is now officially both your circus and your monkey.

The best weapon you have in managing your own reactions is a real understanding of where they come from. So when I am saying these things, it's not in a "nice, letting you off the hook" way, but in a "this is the best understanding we have of brain science" way. I'm going to delve into the brain science a lot more in a bit. Because choosing the right coping skills for you in whatever particular circumstance you are facing means understanding what's really going on and why you need them.

What Exactly Do You Mean by Coping?

Words change in meaning over time and across situations. Sometimes words become so vaguely all-encompassing that we lose a common understanding of their meaning. And if our job here is to figure out how to use coping skills to get better, we need to start with a common understanding of meaning. Defining coping skills relies on a good working understanding of A Bunch of Other Shit™.

So I am going to define certain terms psychologically—what they mean in mental health speak, which can be a far different thing than how words are used in popular culture. And if we are talking about our understanding of the psychological need for coping, then we had better be framing everything at that angle. Otherwise? This would be a useless hot mess of a book. And I aim to write a *useful* hot mess of a book, dammit.

Stress and Distress

The term "stress" has lost all logical meaning, hasn't it? Everything is considered stressful nowadays. And it's entirely probable that everything *is* fucking stressful nowadays. But in a clinical sense, **stress** refers to *any event that requires an output of resources.*

Stress can be good (output of resources to create art or run a race or finish school) or it can be bad (coping with a car accident or an illness or being terminated from a job). Whether the situation is good or bad, we can hit a point where we run out of the resources that we need to cope with the situation.

And that is what **distress** is. *The point of resource depletion.* The point where we need support. Whether you are suffering enormous amounts of emotional pain over a mismatch between your gender and your birth assignment, or whether you are simply aware of this mismatch and that there are things that can be done to bring you into alignment, you could be said to be experiencing psychological distress. You've hit a point where you need resources. It isn't something you can do on your own. It isn't a term that identifies someone as tragically fucked up. It's a clinical term that we understand to mean: *this person needs some help.*

Triggers

Psychologically, **triggers** are events, sensations, images, memories, etc., that facilitate the re-experiencing of any event that overwhelmed our ability to cope. (For those of you playing the home game, yes, that is a quick and dirty definition of trauma.)

Re-experiencing is the big word here, y'all. If you have an unresolved trauma, your brain is wired to literally re-live that trauma in order to protect you in the present once something cues up that traumatic memory (I realize that makes no pragmatic sense, but that's what makes brains assholes).

Ok, so please raise your hand if the overuse of the word trigger in recent years makes you throw up a little bit in your mouth. My hand is raised with you, right now (which totally makes it hard to type, BTW).

Being triggered does not mean being upset or disliking something, or perceiving something or someone as challenging any more than someone disagreeing with you means you are being bullied. Being triggered means you are literally reliving a traumatic event in your body and mind and are not functioning in the present moment or dealing with your present experience.

Coping Skills

"Coping skills" is one of those phrases that we use all the time and have a general idea of what it means, but maybe couldn't define coherently if pressed to do so. For our purposes, I'm going define it as:

*A **conscious** effort to utilize resources to manage or mitigate stressors. The stressors are either internal (in the form of health issues, trauma* *flashbacks, negative self-talk wiring, etc.) or external (bad shit happening, other people's drama, all the crazy shit going on in the world, etc.).*

Coping skills are the tools we use to build up our stress management skills to prevent a freefall into distress. They also help us negotiate with our triggers and mitigate our response if we are triggered.

Y'all with me, right?

Of course, you can totally argue a broader definition here. Coping skills can be *any* way we react to our interpersonal and intrapersonal conflict to self-soothe. The Freuds (both Sigmund and Anna) called these sorts of unconscious coping strategies *defense mechanisms*. More recently, Jungian analyst James Hollis referred to them as *reflexive anxiety management systems*.

But we need to frame coping skills in a more conscious and proactive way. The history of mental health treatment is replete with warnings that if we don't cope with stressors in conscious and productive ways, our brains will create coping skills for us. And they won't be healthy. If we keep bopping along, letting our brain try to figure out its own coping skills, it takes over and starts running the damn show. You might even say this is the genesis of addiction…something we have all dealt with in some form or another. Because, we *need* coping skills. We need resources to combat stress and prevent distress. And we need mechanisms to manage our reactions to being triggered.

We have a pretty good understanding of the brain and how it works, and that understanding is getting better all the time. Brains are just looking to survive. But in the end, we are so much more than embodied brains, sending and receiving messages. That *undefinable more-ness* that makes us our unique selves is the human mind. And you need more than just your brain: it takes the human mind to thrive and heal.

So this book is focused on conscious and proactive coping. It's about being *mind*-focused instead of *brain*-focused. It's centered on how we use coping skills to take our power back in incredibly demanding, frustrating situations. Because, seriously. What the actual literal *fuck* is happening in the world right now???? Sometimes the only power we have is in our own reactions. And if that is the only damn thing we have left, let's hold on as tight as possible to our sanity and humanity.

And, hey. Another note. What about all the stupid shit that gets under our skin? Going back to our definitions of stress and distress, it's not actually stupid. If something requires our resources, big or small, then it just does. And if we are low on resources, spilling our americano (the adult equivalent of letting go of your balloon, dontcha know) can be as distressing as a car accident. Maybe not physically or behaviorally, but emotionally. You feel me?

Side Note For Therapists And Other Treatment Providers: I'm sure you are wondering where I am going with all this and if it will work with the theoretical orientation you operate from. Yo, I hope so! I've intentionally pulled what I have found to be the best and most effective resources from a variety of evidence-based practices and well-established treatment theories. You are gonna find your Cognitive

Behavioral Therapy, Dialectical Behavioral Therapy, Acceptance and Commitment Therapy, Positive Psychology, Mindfulness-Based Stress Reduction, Somatic Experiencing, Relational-Cultural Therapy, and classic Jungian therapy. Eclecticism at its best!

How Do Coping Skills Work?

Coping skills are not woo-woo bullshit. They are mechanisms for managing an altered physiological state and bringing your parasympathetic nervous system back online. They are ways of thinking, feeling, and behaving through a physical state of stress. We cannot control our brain's survival responses, but we can negotiate with them to demonstrate that their situational read is not accurate and that we can manage our current circumstances.

The Science of Coping

At the Brain Level

(Content Warning: Nerdy shit)

First of all, junior high science flashback. Nerves are cells that have special communication functions. They communicate throughout the body as bioelectrical signals. Like, what happens if you touch a hot thing? The nerves in your hand send a message of *"fucking ow!"* to your brain, which then sends a message back saying: *"Well put it the fuck down, then! That's the literal meaning of drop it like it's hot!!!"*

The *vagus nerve* (also called the 10th cranial nerve or Cranial Nerve X which sounds all sci-fi as fuck) is the longest, weirdest, and most complex of the twelve pairs of cranial nerves. The name itself (vagus) comes from the Latin word for "wandering" because this nerve wanders all around the damn body, sending information to organs and tissues. It wouldn't be irrational to say that this particular nerve is an information superhighway.

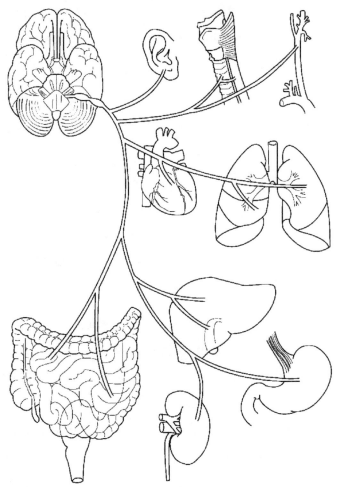

This? The Fancy Fucking Diagram of the Vagus Nerve. So You Can See How the Brain Communicates with Every Major Organ in Your Body. No Pressure to Remain Calm Then, Right?

Ok, now stay with me. There won't be a test, cuz you can't flunk a self-help book. But it will *really* help make all the coping skills information make sense in context.

So your nerves aren't running around like anarchist messengers. They're organized into systems. **Nervous systems** are the networks of the nerve cells and fibers that transmit messages. Nerve cells don't just bop around aimlessly like your useless ex. They are organized into systems that make the messages transmit more efficiently. So that you will, indeed, drop it like it's hot when need be.

Now, human beings have three nervous systems, all of which are autonomic. Autonomic just means they are essentially self-governing. They work involuntarily and are not under conscious control. Because you are *not* allowed at any time to decide whether or not you are going to drop the hot thing. That's the kind of shit that will get you killed. Your body is not interested in negotiation, shit's just getting dropped. You starting to feel me on why this is important info, yeah?

These three nervous systems are known as the sympathetic, parasympathetic, and enteric nervous systems. Again, no test on this. But it's important to understand how they work in relation to each other because pretty recent research has found that these three nervous systems work in ranked order (a hierarchy). This research led a dude named Stephen Porges to develop what he terms *polyvagal theory.* And this is immensely critical to our understanding of how our stress response turns off and on and how coping skills mitigate that response.

In order to understand polyvagal theory, we first need to remember that the fundamental reaction of all animals in the face of a threat is to engage in the fight, flight, freeze response, which is activated (*involuntary*, remember?) by the *sympathetic nervous system*.

The fight, flight, freeze response is critical to our survival. It is activated in the face of a threat or perceived threat, whether it be to our actual, physical safety, the individuals we love and care for, our possessions, or our needs, wants, desires, well-being, and belief systems.

Essentially, anything that challenges the core of who and what we are and who or what belongs to us invokes a protective response.

If we perceive aggression as a means of escape, we will fight. If our instincts tell us we can fight effectively but we can escape, we will flee. If neither of these responses are likely going to be effective, we will freeze.

All of these strategies are purely defensive ones. The intent is not to win against or overwhelm the threat, but to survive. The body's job is to size up the situation and figure out the best means of staying alive. It chooses a strategy based on the information it is receiving and past understanding of the threat. We may move back and forth between strategies as we take in information and gauge our effectiveness at managing the perceived imminent threat. All three responses are part of our defensive, survival instincts.

We read often about the "fight or flight" response, but the freeze response is often left out of literature describing trauma reactions. The freeze response is the one that most human beings are embarrassed about, although it makes just as much sense as a protective strategy as fight and flight do. A freeze response is no more a failure than any other protective coping strategy and is nothing to be ashamed of. Peter Levine states that there are four potential evolutionary survival benefits to the freeze response:

- Most predatory animals won't eat an animal they believe is already dead unless they are really hungry. Most animals have encoded information that meat that is already dead may be spoiled and therefore is a risk to eat.

- It is more difficult for predators to detect prey that is not moving. Immobilization shuts down all movement responses. Even if we are trying to be still and quiet it is difficult to do so unless we have become biochemically immobilized.

- When one animal collapses in a group, this distracts the predator from the rest of the group, allowing their escape.

- The freeze response releases a numbing agent in the body that makes the pain of attack more bearable.

Now obviously, it makes sense that the sympathetic nervous system should not be in charge all the time. It would make us fall apart at the seams pretty quickly (and this is why people who don't have conscious ways to cope with chronic stress *do* fall apart at the seams pretty quickly).

Our second nervous system, the *parasympathetic nervous system*, is the one associated with social relationships and bonding. We're pack animals. We need to connect to other human beings for long-term survival, not just for mating season, and be able to navigate the world without feeling batshit crazy and threatened by our surroundings all the time. Being relaxed and alert is how we best engage with the world around us. This means that when the parasympathetic system is in charge, we are able to connect and communicate and form social relationships because we feel safe to do so.

When Porges said these systems are hierarchical, he was saying that the parasympathetic system is newer and inhibits the older systems. We turn off the fight, flight, freeze response so we can live and work in cooperation and build relationships.

But when something challenges our sense of safety at our lizard brain level, the parasympathetic system goes offline. The sympathetic nervous system is *myelinated,* while the parasympathetic nervous system is not. I know, I know with the science textbook words, but this is actually an important point. Myelination provides insulation...which speeds up the sending of the messages. So the nervous system that is in charge of our stress response works *faster* than the one that is in charge of our chill response.

Both systems operate involuntarily. And the sympathetic nervous system has to be turned off for the parasympathetic nervous system to work, meaning it has to determine that there is no stress or threat and that you are allowed to go about your day. But the sympathetic nervous system is still humming in the background, watching for danger. And it works faster than the chill system, so it will *shut shit down* on a moment's notice.

Any of us with unresolved trauma histories are far more likely to have our parasympathetic systems go offline, putting us into survival mode. I wrote a whole book about how all this goes down in the brain, by the way (*Unfuck Your Brain*, Microcosm Publishing, 2017).

Good coping skills help us manage circumstances without the sympathetic nervous system going into overdrive. Or, even, if you are activated, coping skills can help you de-activate much more quickly (and start to untether the freak-out response that has been ruling your brain for so long). Simply put, good coping skills help keep the parasympathetic nervous system online so we can stay calm and connected. Or they help us manage our sympathetic nervous system activation far more effectively, while getting it turned back off again as soon as possible.

So I said it once. And I really think it merits saying again. These are the facts:

- There are no such things as wrong responses, only adaptive ones

- What you have survived has wired your body to proceed with extreme caution on an unconscious level at all times. This is called staying fucking alive and safe

- You are not choosing to shut down

- This is not a "mental" illness; it is a physiological state of the human body

- You are not crazy; you have adapted to the environment around you with the only information you had at the time...your previous circumstances

Oh, and it's not as important to this conversation, but in order to not leave you hanging: The third nervous system, as mentioned, is the enteric nervous system and it resides in the gastrointestinal tract. It receives feedback from the other two systems but is also able to operate independently of them, as noted in individuals who have severed vagus nerves. It is the reason the stomach is called the second brain. Curious-assed shit, right? I will go into far more detail on that in an upcoming book. So keep that idea on pause for now.

At the Mind Level

(CW: Philosophical Shit)

Getting back to that *brain versus mind* conversation. So if all mammals have this hierarchical response system and all animals, period, are wired to respond to threats with the sympathetic nervous system, why are we the only ones that get all fucked up over it?

This is where I go back to the Jungian analysts. James Hollis writes about how humans experience two types of existential crisis that we consider impactful to our survival. The first is *abandonment*. We crave the structure and reassurance of others in the face of constant change and uncertainty. There are lots of ways we seek out constancy and many people design their lives around this need. Structured religious practice, employment, addictive behavior, and relationships that can be managed through compulsion are some of the big ones.

The other great existential fear that Hollis writes about is *overwhelment.* The world is large and scary and we are relatively powerless against so much of it. This is likely part of the reason we see so many power plays happening in human relationships. When it feels like there is so little we can control, we try to create safety nets of stability and control in our relationships instead.

If these are two core existential crisis triggers, is it any wonder that we can't pull a Taylor Swift and just shake shit off? If something convinces the mind (the *bigger than the sum of its parts* aspect of the brain that makes us uniquely human) that we are disconnected or distressed, it sends us into a tailspin even bigger than the physiological response caused by our brain and body wiring. Humans have the unique capacity for anticipatory distress: that is, making shit up to worry about in the future based on what's happened in the past. This triggers our fear of overwhelment (and, honestly, often our fear of abandonment). Both these things then set off the physiological response of complete brain fuckery, what we just talked about above. Because we are human, we have opposable thumbs and therefore access to the internet and refrigerators. But this also means we also fuck ourselves up on the regular. Helluva trade-off.

Why This Complicated Explanation?

Ok. Shit happens. Then we cope, right? Why is this complicated? Like complicated enough for a whole damn book?

It's complicated because we have these unique human minds that interact with these self-preserving human brains. And we are really good at thinking too much about something or not thinking nearly enough before we act. Essentially, we are super good at getting ourselves in trouble in the following ways:

- We have coping skills but they are unhealthy.

- We *had* coping skills but they've stopped working.

- We don't have enough strategies to fall back on when the skills that usually work don't work.

- We forget to use our strategies in the moment.

- We aren't sure which strategies we should use in which situations.

So how do we resolve these issues and be better at this coping shit?

- *Lots* of fucking practice—when you aren't activated. The therapeutic term for this is "over-learning." Don't practice until you get it right, practice until you are incapable of getting it wrong. As Bruce Lee said, *"Under duress, we do not rise to our expectations, but fall to our level of training."*

- Trying out *lots* of different options. If you have a couple skills that typically work for you, that's awesome. You will be far more successful if you have several more good skills in your back pocket in case your brain goes into asshole mode and doesn't respond to your tried-and-true strategies.

- Code what you are dealing with. I've created four categories of coping skills (more on that in the next section). Two are emotion-focused (meaning they are designed to deal with our internal response to something that has to be lived through, not changed) and two are problem-focused (meaning they are designed to help you navigate the world in a different way to overcome whatever bullshit you are currently having to cope with). Those aren't finite categories. Because you have to manage your own response before you go out to change the world. But being able to identify whether or not a problem-focused coping skill is warranted at any point may help stop you from doing something unproductive. Like trying to forcibly change an unchangeable situation and being frustrated with your lack of success. When your energy would have been better spent learning to managing your own internal reactions to the bullshit around you and being really successful at those emotion-focused coping skills.

Basic Coping, Navy SEAL Style

When mapping out this book, we thought it would be helpful to start with one sort of universal coping skill that is potentially usable by everyone. Easy-peasy, right? Then it really took me awhile to come up with something truly all-encompassing. Until I remembered the Navy SEALs. And how does one, for even one minute, forget the Navy SEALs, FFS?

Backstory time. The Navy works hard to select the most badass, physically fit specimens of humanity for SEAL training. First these recruits have a bunch of "developmental" courses they have to navigate. Then comes the infamous 6-month *Basic Underwater Demolitions/Seal Training* (BUD/S) course.

Despite the Navy's expertise in selecting candidates that are physically up to the task, the dropout rate for individuals attending SEAL school is really damn high (like 75% high). After years of this, the Navy commissioned psychologists to figure out what was different about the 25% that succeeded. And they found, unsurprising, that it was a form of mental ability, not of physical ability. There were four essential abilities that were later termed "The Four Pillars of Mental Toughness" and the ideas within it really carry all the coping skill categories that I listed above. The four pillars represent a seriously well-woven set of coping skills we can all learn from.

Pillar One: Very Short Term and Very Specific Goal Setting

Goals that are going to take a while or are sort of vaguely nebulous are recipes for disaster. We need a quantifiable ending and we need to see it right up ahead. Navy SEALs who focused on getting through the training activity at hand rather than the course overall were far more successful in finishing the entire program. "OK, let me get through this assignment, I can always quit after," is literally how I talked myself through my doctoral program, y'all.

Pillar Two: Positive Mental Visualization

This means mentally watching yourself successfully complete the task you set out to accomplish or endure the bullshit you need to endure. We are wired for the negative as a species survival skill, which means we visualize failure, which leads to the brain saying *abort mission*. We can replace that automatic response with a positive walk-through and a successful outcome. And we are far more likely to make that happen if we do.

Pillar Three: Positive Self-Talk

Check this shit out: our rate of inner dialogue is far higher than our capacity for verbal speech. It's actually been clocked at 4000 words a minute! And again, since we are wired for the negative, we tend to speechify negative ideas. Instead, if we intentionally use positive self-talk, mantras, and encouragement we are far more likely to succeed. Remind yourself this ain't no thang compared to everything else you've been through. And hell, your survival rate thus far is 100% so the odds are in your favor, rock star.

Pillar Four: Managing Self Arousal

Managing our cortisol and adrenaline production is a huge part of coping in general. Techniques that keep the body calm in turn keep the feeling-thoughts better managed. Breathing techniques are a big part of that, which is why I include different variations of them in so much of what I write. One of the basic ones that SEALs use is a simple 4x4 technique. In for four, then out for four. It's less complicated than some of the others, which makes it easier to use when your brain and body are going into absolute panic mode (such as when, during BUD/S training, candidates have their wrists and ankles tied before they are dumped into a pool to simulate drowning and the breathing part doesn't work so good anymore). Breathing techniques can help us so much in immediate moments of utter terror. Because it is such good medicine for many circumstances, a slightly more enhanced version of SEAL breathing is included as one of my favorite *live through this* skills in the next part of the book.

Types of Coping Skills

There are eleventy billion ways to define and categorize coping skills. Or at least, it felt that way when I was reading up on them. None of these ways of conceptualizing coping quite fit how *I* view the coping process, however, so I decided to create my own framework. Way to make life difficult for myself, right?

Why was I so determined to do that and why are you going to see a category list that didn't exist until this one fell into place in my brain while driving to work one morning? Many of the coping skills categories that other writers and theorists have created separate out cognitive coping skills from emotional coping skills. That's hardly useful when they both inform each other in a continuous feedback loop.

We are feeling beings more than we are thinking beings. We feel first, and that informs our thoughts. Some counseling theories state that you can absolutely never separate the two at all, even going so far as to refer to them as one entity: *feeling-thoughts*. So any coping skills worth a shit are going to target both the thought and the feeling.

Other categorizations that make me cranky include separating coping skills into categories like "helpful" and "unhelpful." Very few coping skills exist in a finite dichotomy of good or bad, so me pretending otherwise while operating as the decider is bullshit. Other categorizations I found in the literature tend to be more limited in scope, like focusing on an individual's ability to engage in a job that helps them feel they are having a positive impact in the world. Occupation as its own coping skill category? As we so eloquently say at my house, *fucking really*? Having that kind of job is a rare privilege (I know because I *do* have that kind of job), and most of us have to find other ways to feel we are making a positive impact on the world around us.

So here is the breakdown I came up with, based on how the brain works (because, science) coupled with the fact that reality is quite often a dumpster fire (because, society). The presumption that we all have the luxury of being proactive world-changers is cruel. And insisting otherwise becomes a mechanism for mind-fucking people into thinking they are complete failures at managing the human condition. So I created my coping skill categories based on how the world actually works.

Live Through This **Skills**—These are for when the shit hits the fan and the only power you have lies in your own response. It's survival without losing your damn mind time.

Internal Judo **Skills**—Here is where we go a bit deeper, and change our relationship with the bullshit in our own mind. How do we make space with what's going on in our minds that gives us more of a sense of control but without blowing smoke up our own asses?

Mitigate the Bullshit **Skills**—Here is where we get more behavior-oriented. How can we structure what we do to create better outcomes in response to the craziness around us?

Find The Pony Skills—Here are the society-changing, expert-level coping skills that can be done without actual world domination. The secret bonus part is that it's stuff that makes the other stuff easier to do as well, so you get to be a living saint *and* selfish as fuck at the same time.

And finally, I've included a long list of uncategorized quick-n-dirty coping skills that you can try on. It's good to have a bunch of random tools in your back pocket when you are blindsided with some bullshit and don't have the juice to slip into a *mettā* meditation or some such saintly shit. Survival in the short term is how we win in the long term, so let's get to it!

Live Through This Skills

This is the feeling-thoughts management category. It's the catch-all for all the ways we just manage our own activation and responses to whatever stress, grossness, and fuckery that's been dished out to us without completely losing our minds. These are what therapists usually call "distress tolerance" skills.

These skills are about managing shitty feeling-thoughts. Not trying to unpack them or challenge them or change them in any way. Just to go, *"Oh yeah, this feels like shit. But I can deal with this. Feeling-thoughts are just information from my body that bad shit is going down. They won't last forever. I can pay attention to them without falling apart."*

Grounding Techniques

Grounding techniques are one of those things I yammer on about all the damn time. Because they *work* and are *simple* and help us remain in the present moment in our bodies, and be aware of our surroundings. If you are a trauma survivor (and hey there, aren't we all??) then it's really easy to start reliving a past experience when shit is getting tough in the present. Grounding techniques are one of those can-do-anywhere coping skills that cost nothing and don't make you look obviously odd if you are using them while sitting on the bus.

Mental Grounding

Mental grounding techniques are intended to keep you in the present moment by focusing on your current situation and surroundings. Anything that helps you remind yourself of where you are in the moment and that you have more control over your feeling-thoughts even though your stress reaction has been tripped.

- Use a phrase or mantra that is soothing to you. Navy SEAL positive self talk, style. It could be "I got this" or "This is temporary" or "This may pass like a fucking kidney stone, but it *will* pass." Whatever works for you.

- Play a categories game with yourself. Name all your favorite shows, movies, books, songs, etc. The point is to draw from semantic memory instead of emotional memory.

- Describe something in great detail that is attached to the present moment. It may be all the colors you can see in front of you or an article you are holding in your hand.

- Go over your schedule in your mind, or the steps it takes to complete an activity you do well. This is accessing procedural memory, which is a declarative form of memory just like semantic memory...which helps you detach from the emotional memory being triggered.

Physical Grounding

It's the most amazing magic trick ever when we first realize as children that we can check out mentally from where we are physically. Teacher droning on and on? Totally just mentally escape to the playground. Then as we get older we realize *"Oh, shit! Now I'm doing this automatically! Even when I don't wanna! How do I get back in my body?"* Physical grounding techniques do just that thing.

- Notice your breath. Just the physical in and out breathing experience. When your mind starts to wander, go back to the breath.

- Walk mindfully. Notice every step you take and the feeling when your foot connects to the earth. If your mind starts wandering away from you, you can always try holding a teaspoon of water while walking and focus on not spilling the water.

- Touch objects around you.

- Jump up and down.

- Eat something mindfully, attending to the flavors and textures.

- Make sure your feet are touching the floor. Try taking off your shoes and feeling the ground beneath you.

- If someone else touching you feels safe, have them put their hands on your shoulders and remind you to ground back in your body.

Square Breathing

Who else learned to breathe by sucking in their stomachs and filling their lungs deeply? Didn't we all? Isn't it a great irony (in the Alanis Morissette sense of the word) that this is exactly the opposite of how you should use breathing to calm yourself down? In order to get the most calming effect and encourage our brain waves to operate in alpha state (relaxed and focused), we should breathe from our bellies. If you've never done that before, lay down and put a stuffed animal or something else lightweight on your stomach and breathe deeply enough to see it move. That's the kind of breathing that is a functional coping skill.

Square breathing comes from dialectical behavior therapy, and is a fairly simple expansion of the Navy SEAL breathing technique mentioned above.

- Breathe in for a count of four.

- Hold it for a count of four.

- Breathe out for a count of four.

- And hold one more time for a count of four.

Then repeat the sequence three more times (and yes, you did the math right...for a total of *four*). You can totally do it longer than that if it's helping you. But give it at least a full cycle of four before checking in on your stress level.

Pendulation and Titration

The typical trauma response is this one:

Something acts as a trigger, either an external event or a memory, and your trauma response is *activated*. You start noticing thoughts, feelings, sensations, and physical responses associated with the trauma. These aren't positive sensations, so you go from just fine to totally dysregulated in under a minute, right?

Along with emotions, we also experience *sensations*. Sensations are how things present in our body. Sensations language helps us recognize what's going on in our body, even when words fail. (And there's a reason words fail; the region of the brain responsible for language, known as Broca's area, goes inactive in a trauma response.) Once we start to connect to the sensations we feel when our trauma response is triggered, we can better control our response.

Pendulation work was developed by Peter Levine (who wrote *Waking The Tiger,* among other books), whose work is focused on the somatic experience of trauma. That is, *how we hold trauma in our body.*

Pendulation starts with connecting to the sensations we feel in our body, especially when you are activated. But rather than staying in that place, you identify a space of calmness and safety. It's often referred to as an oasis (think of where you draw water from in the desert, when you are dying of thirst), a pool of resources, or your natural supports.

Pendulation is the action of teaching yourself to move in and out of the activated sensations into your space of calmness. The idea is that we all have a safe space inside ourselves that we can draw strength from if we remember it's there. And it can help you gain mastery over the activation and help you learn to tolerate the sensations and feelings associated with activation for longer periods of time. And titration operates within that framework as a way of managing the flow. Trauma is too much, too fast, all at once. And titration is a way of managing all our feels one baby step at a time. It is our conscious effort to slow everything down so we can deal with it in manageable chunks.

So when you start recognizing that you are activated, you can let yourself feel the negatives, and then remind yourself that you can intentionally move to your space of calmness and gather resources to process and release your experiences piece by piece.

Once you start to find ways to tolerate your activation, it no longer owns you. It no longer hijacks the entirety of your being, which means you are able to start managing your responses, operate from your prefrontal cortex again, and the activation starts to dissipate.

Pendulation Exercise

It sounds weird until you try it a couple of times, so here is a step-by-step guide. And if you don't want to write in a perfectly lovely book, you can download my worksheet version of this exercise from my website (faithgharper. com).

Start by scanning your body to figure out which areas feel safe and secure for you and which tend to get activated when you are stressed. I tend to feel stress in my stomach, others feel it in their neck and shoulders, for example. Try using the following color codes to mark where you feel the most activated (anxious, angry, upset) in your body, and where you feel the most calm. This information will help you deliberately connect to, and feel calmer during, times you are highly activated by intentionally stepping into your calm space until the highest level sensations are able to discharge and dissipate.

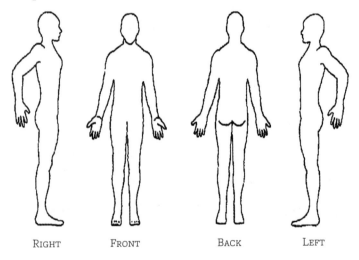

RIGHT   FRONT   BACK   LEFT

Red – The places that feel high-range activated

Orange – The places that feel medium-range activated

Yellow – The places that feel low-range activated

Green – The places that feel neutral

Blue – The places that feel calm

You may not be really sure where your places are, especially if you have disassociated from your body sensations in order to get through life without a total breakdown. That's entirely OK, and makes perfect sense...but here is your chance to start trying to connect to those sensations throughout the days and weeks ahead. If you have a therapist you are working with, you can incorporate this work into therapy.

Once you have a good idea of where you feel most safe in your body and where you feel most activated, the pendulation exercise is designed to help you move back and forth so you can experience feeling intense emotions without having them completely take over.

You start with the part of your body that feels safe (the oasis space). For me, that's always my chest...in my heart and in my breath. Then you move your awareness into the activated space. For me, that would be my stomach, like I mentioned. Approach the activated space gently. With neutrality and curiosity about the experience, rather than anxiety, anger, embarrassment and shame. For example:

Hey there stomach, you're upset with me today. I can tell. I'm aware. I'm aware. Thank you for letting me know. I want you to feel safe, but you don't get to take over and be in charge.

Then you move back to the safe space...in your body. For me (again), it's a returning to my breath.

It sounds woo-woo, but really all you're doing is teaching your brain to manage the sensations in your body. To invite the presence into consciousness without letting them go into hostile takeover mode. And learning to experience them without a constant sense of being overwhelmed.

The rhythm of moving back and forth through internal states will influence the vagus nerve and the connective tissue throughout your body, which will help flush out the stress hormones and help turn off the physiological trigger response that was activated in you.

1) When you find yourself activated notice where it is in your body. Do you feel tense? Shakey? Completely numb?

2) Where in your body do you feel safest or at least neutral?

3) Practice focusing on the activated feelings then moving slowly to focus on the safer feelings. As you practice and feel in control of the movement, you can spend more time on the activated feelings, showing yourself that they are manageable and will dissipate.

Open Hand/Closed Hand

This is a far simpler body awareness exercise that works really well if the pendulation and titration exercise is either too much to handle or too complicated to figure out. And because you are focusing on your hands, you are less likely to activate your sympathetic system through the vagus nerve, therefore less likely to accidentally becoming triggered.

1) Hold out one of your hands. It doesn't matter which one but pay attention to your natural inclination.

2) Hold it in the air, without letting it rest against another surface (like your leg or the table in front of you), if you are able to do so without pain.

3) Open the palm of your hand up, facing back towards you so you have the palm of your hand directly in your line of sight.

4) While watching your hand, slowly make it into a fist. Notice the difference in the sensation from what it felt like open and what it feels like closed.

5) Maintaining eye contact, open your hand back up.

6) Now close your eyes and repeat this sequence. Notice what it feels like from the inside (the closing and opening of your hand into a fist).

What felt different? How did your awareness of the experience change once you were entirely dependent on your internal sense messages? Was it disconcerting at any point? Comforting? Did anything shift or feel different in how you connect with your body?

INHALE

EXHALE

Internal Judo Skills

I stole this term from Aaron Sapp, my ever-patient friend and collaborator. The skills in this category are about evaluating our internal responses (thoughts or feelings). While everything we feel is real, it may not always reflect reality. And even if your internal thought process represents the truthiest truth in the history of all that is accurate about the universe, that doesn't mean that you are entirely stuck with the exact story you've got going on right now. Feeling-thoughts may be accurate, but not the least bit fucking helpful.

These skills are the ones where you recognize your feeling-thoughts and work to unpack them a bit. Or reframe them just enough to create some breathing room. Sometimes coping means recognizing the fuckery going on but distancing ourselves from it mentally.

Prayer and Meditation

These are the things that people tell me over and over are their two biggest coping skills. You may be rolling your eyes up in your head at me over this one, I know. Prayer? I don't do religion. Meditate? I sure as hell don't have time to sit and "ommmm" for an hour. *Next skill, please!*

But let's unpack these skills before you decide they're not for you. You want to be able to be fully informed before telling me to fuck off, right?

The reason that both prayer and meditation feel weird and icky for people is that they are tied, intrinsically, to spirituality. And so many people have had really fucked up experiences with one of the common expressions of spirituality...organized religion. Even though I was raised by theological scholars who encouraged healthy skepticism of bullshit coupled with a doctrine of inclusivity and acceptance, I still had plenty of church going experiences that left me angry, sad, and disconnected. After all, my parents were fighting against a huge tsunami of religion as a mechanism of toxic control, rather than an impetus for love, care, and action. And while I wasn't anti-religion, I wasn't sure where I fit into some sort of religious practice.

Then spirituality (and to some extent, the organization of spirituality into religious practice) came up over and over and *over* again in my dissertation research. I couldn't hide from my own damn data. And while trying to come up with a way to categorize how we think about and use spirituality and religion in our lives, I bumped into Geral Blanchard's definition of spirituality. He keeps it simple, and simple is what I needed: **spirituality is just *purposeful belonging.***

Our fundamental mechanisms of invoking this purposeful belonging are prayer and meditation. I know this still sounds very incense, chanting, and woo-woo... but I've had several people tell me since the Coping Skills zine this book is based on first came out, that they had a huge shift in their thinking with how I presented my understanding of prayer and meditation.

Essentially, what we have agreed, culturally, to define as **prayer** is just *talking to*. Speaking either to ourselves or something bigger than ourselves (God, YHWH, Higher Power, or whomever you speak to) about our wants, needs, desires, and intentions. Human beings are storytellers, after all. We even tell ourselves stories in our sleep, though we call it dreaming. Talking through our situation in this manner can be far more powerful than talking to a friend, family member, or therapist. It's a grounding experience that helps us be more aware of our thoughts, feelings, and behaviors.

So what's mediation, then? **Meditation** is *listening to*. Meditation is the process of quieting ourselves down enough to hear what's going on inside us. Our minds are brilliant at creating endless amounts of chatter that we often talk back to without listening first. Meditation doesn't require a red cushion, a saffron robe, and a shaved head (unless that works for you). It just means a willingness to hear yourself before you start arguing back.

Settle in and pay attention. See what you find out.

Escapism

If prayer and meditation are a way of being in the present moment, escapism is a way of pulling back from an untenable situation without getting muddled up in the past. OK, what's the difference, fancy doctor lady? **Escapism** is a conscious move into another world for a while. It could be through guided imagery, a wonderful book, moving music, or binge-watching *Grace and Frankie* on Netflix.

Escapism is intentionally moving to another space in a mental and emotional way (but of course you may go all balls out and take a vacay… that works too). It gives you a chance to soothe your tired self without getting trapped in a nasty cycle of perseverating on memories. Seriously. Go to the thrift store and buy up all the *Babysitter's Club* books (or whatever you loved to read as a kid), run a bubble bath, and escape the fuck up outta this mess.

The important thing is that the escapism be proactive rather than passive. A lot of people who struggle with depression report spending a ton of time sitting around and watching TV... and report that they don't feel any better for doing so. To use terms borrowed from cognitive behavior therapy, we are looking for things that provide a sense of pleasure and maybe even mastery.

One of the escapism ideas I talked about above is guided imagery. I've found that people get confused about guided imagery and meditation, thinking they are essentially the same thing. In fact, guided imagery is pretty much the opposite of meditation but still a very positive coping skill. Guided imagery is a form of storytelling. It is the use of words (and sometimes music and other soothing sounds) to invoke and guide you to a calm, focused, and relaxed state. Oftentimes you're encouraged to use your imagination to picture yourself somewhere calming, like on a beach or in the woods. It's a form of intentional and healthy distraction (escapism) from your current stressful situation.

If you are ruminating and upset and worried for the future (the clinical term is anticipatory distress), then guided imagery helps you refocus your imagination to something that is calming and positive.

Research demonstrates that guided imagery, if done properly, calms our flooding of stress hormones (therefore our emotional turmoil) and helps us manage physical pain by activating our subconscious processes as well as our conscious ones. "Properly" means including the following elements identified by licensed social worker Belleruth Naparstek, one of the first people to utilize guided imagery as a clinical intervention. Her categories, with my brief interpretation of each, are listed below.

- *The Mind-Body Connection:* Guided imagery puts the entirety of your body into the image. The subconscious only understands the present tense, and will relate to sensory cues. Things that help you feel, hear, see, smell, and taste will activate all the right "pay attention" cues in us.

- *The Altered State:* By engaging our entire body in guided imagery we are essentially invoking a form of self-hypnosis. This focused state helps us connect to our creativity and intuition while managing our negative thoughts and feelings. Our brain waves literally change our heartbeat, our breathing patterns, etc.

- *Locus of Control:* Good guided imagery puts *you* in charge of the action. You are being guided, but you are the one doing the real movement in your mind and it is toward a direction that serves your healing and growth.

Belleruth's website HealthJourneys.com has a ton of guided imagery audio files that follow these principles. There are also lots of great guided imagery sessions on YouTube and other places on the web. Check some out, keeping in mind the healing elements mentioned above!

Self-Compassion

OK, let's be honest. It's just us here, after all, right? How do you talk to yourself when you fuck up or even think you might have fucked up or that you might fuck up in the future? What kind of nasty things do you say? What tends to trigger that experience for you? How well do you connect to others after shitting all over yourself? Kristen Neff (author of the literal book on *Self-Compassion*) says: "If you are continually judging and criticizing yourself while trying to be kind to others, you are drawing artificial boundaries and distinctions that only lead to feelings of separation and isolation."

Instead, treat yourself like you would your best friend. What if they had fucked up hardcore? You would be compassionate, wouldn't you? You wouldn't let them off the hook, but you would help them take responsibility, try to fix the mess they made, and remind them that they are a human being, after all. And human beings fail.

Give yourself the same compassion you would give someone you love. Instead of, "I can't believe that bullshit you pulled, why on Earth are you even on this planet????"

try, "Wow, OK, so that didn't work out. Everything went sideways. I need to figure out the best thing to do now to try to fix as much as possible. And figure out why it went sideways so I can try to avoid it happening again. I feel like shit right now, but I can learn from this and fail differently and fail better next time."

Give Yourself Five Minutes to Channel Your Inner Veruca Salt

Veruca Salt is the horrible child from *Charlie and The Chocolate Factory*. Remember her? Demanding that all eyes be on her and that she get all that she wishes, Veruca gets in the way of what really matters because she takes over.

Anxiety can become the emotional equivalent of Veruca Salt, taking over everything. And sometimes the best way to treat it is to give in. The official therapeutic term for this is *paradoxical intention.*

The idea behind paradoxical intention is: *what you resist persists*. And if you intentionally invoke what is causing you so much anxiety, it loses its power. I like to set a time limit, which helps you know there is something to pull you back from the anxiety pit you are entering. Five minutes to do *nothing* but think of the thing causing anxiety. Nothing else. Just be anxious. But unlike being a total bitch like Veruca, (and end up falling down a garbage chute), approach what you are feeling with acceptance. And curiosity. And neutrality. It's just what you feel, right? Not good or bad. And those emotions may be relaying some important information to you, if you open yourself up to really listening to yourself.

And if it's just useless mental jibber-jabber, that's OK, too. I've found I'm really over myself and my bullshit after about three minutes.

Curiosity and Neutrality

We tend to label things as good or bad, wanted or unwanted. Approaching life with curiosity and neutrality shuts up our internal judge and jury. **Curiosity** means just applying the question "Oh, interesting, I wonder where that is coming from?" to both the behaviors of others, and our own thoughts and feelings. It allows us to pay attention and look for clues that explain what's going on.

Often clients will come in and tell me a story, ending it with *"... and they totally did XXX for YYY reason!"* My response is usually to the tune of *"Oh, wow. Well you know them better than I do, but when you were telling me the story I couldn't help but wonder if they were doing XXX for another reason, such as... "* It's tough, when you are actively mad at someone, not to ascribe malicious intent to their behavior. But truly, not everyone is going around plotting and scheming like a cartoon villain. It doesn't change the outcome of the behavior, but it may make coping with the behavior far easier...and help facilitate a conversation where it doesn't happen again.

Neutrality is a mental-shifting exercise that really helps with all behaviors and intentions, but especially your own. When you can't find the good in a situation, and you have no energy for active curiosity, you can actively label it as neutral and move on. It's not good or bad, *it just is what it is*. It exists and you are going to contend with it. You don't have to take ownership of it as being directed toward making your life difficult or some repayment of your karmic debt. And if it is inward negative messaging that you can't switch off? Start by trying to have a more neutral interaction with yourself. Positive may be difficult if you have years of negative programming. Neutral will give you a measure of relief and may be far more doable in the present.

Mitigate the Bullshit Skills

These are behavioral coping skills: The practical things you can do to manage and tolerate whatever shit is going on. Not by managing your own internal processes, but by better managing whatever it is that you are squaring off against. But do it productively. Don't put in an UberEats order for donuts just yet. We're going for pragmatic action plans that help you boss through fucked up situations.

Clarification Exercise: What Problem Are You Trying To Solve?

Are you bumped up against an unsolvable problem? Maybe it's the problem itself, not your inability to find a solution. Consider the case of the non-morning person.

No matter how many alarms he sets, he can't get up on time. If he could just find that one, loud alarm clock that he could hang up out of reach to ensure he gets to work by 8 am. Except maybe the real problem that needs to be solved is why is he not getting enough rest? Is he getting to bed early enough? How is his quality of sleep? Does he have sleep apnea so he is perpetually exhausted? The problem to be solved is not about another alarm clock purchase. The problem is the lack of adequate rest.

The media pushback about the marketing of "Lady Doritos" is another good example. The company got huge backlash for saying that women don't like chips that are loud, messy, and hard to carry. Women everywhere banded together with an unified message of "lol, fuck off." Gendering differences in chip consumption was not a problem to be solved. Creating an alternate product that all people could use to assist in portability for meals and snacks on the go was the problem that needed to be solved. And the exact same snack, marketed thusly, may have done fantastically well. (Though, for the record, the crumbs at the bottom are always my favorite... and I wouldn't want anything that didn't have them.)

So when trying to manage some life bullshittery, check in to make sure you are solving the right problem before you get started on the solving part. I mean seriously, did we really need Lady Doritos? In the zine that this book is based on, I called it looking at the problem with sideways eyes. Literally shift your perspective and ask others for theirs. Some super fancy tips:

1) Ask yourself: is your current problem unsolvable? If so, time to stop perseverating on trying to solve it!

2) Have you tried solving a different problem yet? Something that might get you to a more manageable place, that's related to this scenario but has a different focus? If no, let's try that!

3) If you can, collect yourself one other person. Maybe two. Not a group. Groups creates chaos and distractions. Look for people you

trust and respect but who have a different worldview than you. Different perspectives are helpful.

4) Ask questions. Literally just ask questions. No solution offering or suggestions. Just questions associated with your situation.

5) And collect them and write them down.

6) Review your questions. Sort them into categories based on your emerging themes. What sort of categories are taking shape? Can any of these categories be distilled down into fewer questions? Maybe one singular question?

7) Do any of these questions seem approachable as possibly solvable? Mark those. Circle, highlight, whatever.

8) Any emerging themes again? Anything that can be distilled down into less questions or a singular question?

9) Ask for feedback from others if you can. Even if no one participated in the process up until this point. What do they notice? Do they see anything missing, question-wise?

10) From the solvable list, pick a question you are ready to tackle. Dump out what you were trying to resolve and focus on this one instead. *Now* brainstorm ideas for resolution.

Building Structure Within Chaos: Create Your Ladder

When your ability to manage huge, incoming waves of bullshit is compromised for *whatever* reason, this is a fantastic technique for getting through days and weeks of really stressful times. Maybe you are dealing with a chronic health condition (whether physical, mental, or both). Maybe you are newly in recovery. Maybe you are just going through a truly awful period in your life with significant, shitty changes.

And hell, even if you have good change going on, it can still be intensely stressful. Maybe you're moving, going back to school, got a promotion, getting married, or having a baby. It seems shitty and unfair to compare it to someone going through cancer treatment and it's definitely not near as bad. But higher levels of stress for any reason mean coping skill activation time.

Building a system of self-care strategies (I mean, aren't those coping skills, too??) that help you mitigate ongoing stress can really help you get through the type of issue that is more marathon than sprint. We've read in articles (or seen on insta) tributes to stuff like *"a good skin care routine will totally change your life!"* I mean, not in and of itself. That's bypassing the depth of how fucked up shit can be. No one has loved me less because I had a zit on my chin. And not having a zit didn't make a shitty boss less shitty.

But. *But.* Self-care strategies can build on each other in a way that helps support your ability to cope. Think of each of your self-care strategies as rungs on a ladder. You are climbing this ladder out of stress and overwhelm into stability. Think about what a quality daily routine looks like for you, and list them in the sequential order that works best for you. For example, some people feel best when they shower first thing. My husband likes to shower later in the day, after he has done grubby work like dishes, or yard work, or cat boxes. Makes total sense, right? They may not be empirically important but they are important to *your* day. Maybe your routine includes a butter coffee and puppy snuggles. It's your list so you define what's important.

The great thing about this image, is you will really pay attention to how important all of these activities are to your well-being because each one is a step up and out. If you miss a rung, you feel the difference in your balance immediately. The next step is that much harder to take. And if you start pulling out lots of rungs willy-nilly? You are either hanging on for dear life with no real movement upward *or you are going to fall.*

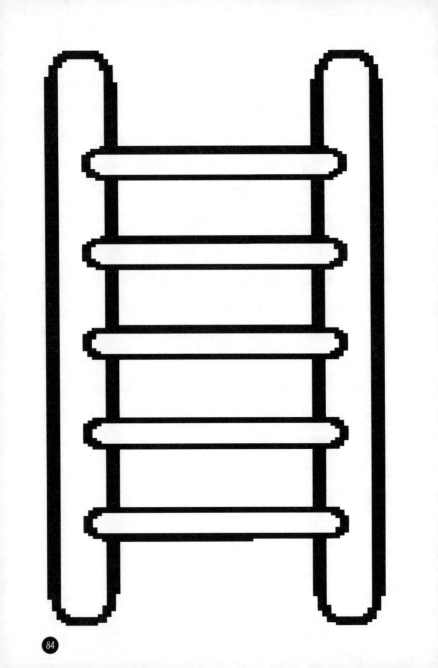

The Grenade Test

Quick question. Are the actions you are taking helpful to your relationships? No matter how shitty someone is, responding in kind is essentially lobbing a grenade over the wall. The grenade test is when you step back and ask yourself: is what you are about to say or do akin to pitching a grenade at the other person, and at the relationship itself?

I'm not talking about *allowing* bad behavior from others, I'm talking about *retaliating* against others for their bad behavior. If people throw grenades at you, replace the pin and hand it back. That may look something like saying "Hey, that's hurtful and completely not helpful to what we are trying to resolve here. Can we have a productive conversation, or do we need to parking lot this chat until we can respond to each other without striking out?" It may also look like excusing yourself from a diatribe set upon you. But what it *doesn't* look like is fighting back. You don't have to throw a grenade in retaliation to one thrown at you. If you engage in a grenade war, nothing ever gets better because you are still interacting in a way that amplifies the exchange.

Instead you are taking a step back before reacting and deciding if you're reacting in a way that serves to make the relationship stronger in the long run. Refusing to fight with someone clearly trying to pick a fight better serves the relationship. Adding context to their assholery rather than reacting with your own better serves the relationship. Setting a boundary about behavior you will not accept *totally* serves the relationship. Punching back just because you got punched does not.

Ask yourself, what will this response accomplish both in the short and long term. If the answer is *"I'm gonna let a motherfucker know he messed with the wrong person this time!"* what does that serve to accomplish in the long term? What if this is your partner, a family member, a dear friend?

You can't force other people to treat you the way you want to be treated (or the way you want the world to be treated), but you can change how you respond. How much power do you want to give them? Do you want to carry that around forever? I don't mean letting people get away with douchebaggery, but I do mean not giving them the power of owning your headspace. Responding appropriately doesn't mean responding with equal vengeance. Or seething and carrying all those intense, negative feelings for days. You aren't punishing other people with your anger, not really. You're mostly just punishing yourself.

Have Some Fun, FFS

We need to laugh. We *need* to laugh, y'all.

Laughing is good for us emotionally, right? It decreases stress hormones in the body and helps us think more creatively. Did you also know it has direct physical benefits as well? Like immediate benefits, not just the reducing of wear and tear on the body by reducing stress hormones. It also relaxes our muscles, strengthens our heart and lungs, and decreases physical pain.

Be an epic goofball. Seriously. Praise be to Pokemon Go for getting people out and doing stuff again. For about five minutes, Pokemon Go was beating out porn in internet usage. That's crazy awesome. Who knows what the fuck the new hot thing will be by the time you are reading this book, but I am all in for anything that gives us permission to be epic goofballs. I will talk in a crazy accent, wear weird t-shirts (I love buying t-shirts from the boys' section of the store) to work (the benefit of being self-employed... I set the dress code), dance with my waiter in the middle of the restaurant (thanks, Paul!), and have my husband (a deeply patient man) push me through the grocery store parking lot while I stand on the shopping cart.

Because sometimes we just *need* to laugh. Taking a minute to step out of everything heavy and remember that life can also be enjoyable gives us the perspective and energy we need to fight another day.

The Pomodoro Technique

The entrepreneur Francesco Cirillo created The *Pomodoro Technique* as a method of task management in the face of overwhelment. It's easy AF, y'all. The

Pomodoro in question is the little kitchen timer that looks like a tomato. You've totally seen it before. You break down whatever bullshittery you have to tackle into chunks of time that are manageable for an adult attention span with breaks added in for relief. You set your timer for 25 minutes and work. Then you take a five-minute break. After four Pomodoro cycles you take a longer break.

You start training yourself into better focus, concentration, and time management by working in sprints rather than marathons, with built in breaks to help you maintain motivation. It doesn't make completely impossible goals suddenly magically attainable, but it *can* help you keep from mind-fucking yourself into thinking that you won't finish something that is actually pretty doable. If nothing else, it's a really good system for giving something your best shot so you can be proud you were proactive and tried your damn ass off.

Find the Pony Skills

You know those people who fall in a pile of shit but somehow manage to find the pony? They aren't just Pollyanna motherfuckers pretending that everything has greater meaning. They are doing something bigger than that. They are taking the reality of their situation and wringing whatever good they can from it. They are saying, *fuck off world, I'm a survivor*. And this is actually using a brilliant fucking coping skill. Finding greater meaning in horrible circumstances allows you to transcend your current environment and leave the world a better place through your advocacy and action.

My favorite book of all time is Viktor Frankl's *Man's Search For Meaning*. His experience as a concentration camp survivor led to a form of therapy known as logotherapy. In a nutshell, he realized that finding meaning can be a fundamental part of our emotional healing. Some coping skills can be transformative as fuck. And that's so badass, don't you think?

Creation

Put something new in the world that didn't exist before. Destruction, as you well know, is not an abstraction. It's a very real entity we cope with on a daily basis. People destroy. They destroy physical structures. They destroy other living beings. They destroy in ways that cannot be measured physically but are physical nonetheless.

Anyone who has laid down on the floor from the sheer weight of the awfulness of life can tell you that grief and loss are very real, physical things... and the reason we can't measure them is because they're far too large for any scale. What is the antithesis of destruction? Creation.

When other people out there in the world take away from you, create back. There really is no such thing as a "self," no matter what they told you in your psychology classes. Selfhood is a modern, western concept of the human experience that has nothing to do with how people really navigate the world. We don't stand alone on a hilltop. We do, however, have individual voices.

We have a mechanism of communication about everything we think, feel, say, and do. Creation is the sharing of that voice. You can paint a canvas, knit a scarf, play a song, plant a tree, or bake a cake. You can write and write and write and write. On your website, your Facebook, or the back of a napkin at a coffee shop. Creation in the face of destruction doesn't mitigate the loss, but it does help us take back power when we feel completely out of control. You are allowed your voice in the world.

The Tombstone Test

Another easy task, with a perhaps more complicated answer. What do you want to see written on your tombstone? Are the things you are doing right now moving you toward that epitaph?

This is another way of asking if what you are doing right now is the way you want to be remembered. If not, how can you shift your behavior so that you are still caring for yourself and maintaining good boundaries but presenting your best self to the world in the process?

Change the Fucking World

My mom used to make gentle fun of my brother. "Bless his heart, he still thinks he can change the world." My response? "Well, those are the people who usually do." Nothing ever got changed by sitting around, hoping that people come to their senses and make better choices. Nobody has gained rights by sitting around patiently waiting for someone to notice that they were getting fucked over.

Anne Lamott writes that when the world overwhelms her, she starts writing checks and planting bulbs. The checks she writes are to organizations doing good work in the world. The ones combating the evil that feels overwhelming to her. Planting bulbs is an investment in the future. Flowers like tulips start as hardy bulbs.

They are planted in the Fall, and thrive on spending the cold winter in the ground before flowering in the Spring. Planting bulbs acts as a physical reminder that we can survive tough times and bloom anyway.

Things change when we change them. Or, at the very least, we empower ourselves to fucking *try*. I don't know about you, but I'm not about to sit by and do nothing when the world is on fire. I'll find a bucket of water. Or spit on it if that's all I got. But I always feel far better when I try to make things better.

If I'm going down, it's not with an attitude of fatalism and nihilism. I'm fighting each step of the way.

Do Something Nice for Someone

Did you know studies show that doing something nice for someone else activates our reward centers even more than when we do something nice for ourselves? For reals. I'm not saying you can't get yourself a new pair of kicks after a tough week but consider what you can do for someone else out there who is probably also having a shitty time.

Can you bring muffins in to share with everyone you work with? Compliment a stranger on their cool t-shirt? Shoot hoops with the kids in the neighborhood? Whenever you do something for someone else, you are inviting them into your circle of self-care. And maybe you're giving them permission to start taking better care of themselves and improve their own coping skills.

Practice Compassion and Loving-Kindness

We talked about self-compassion, right? And about how compassion starts at home, with our own humanity. Now that we are working on that, we are going to start working on expanding that out to others, and complementing that practice with loving-kindness.

Compassion toward others means wishing that all others be free from suffering. As you work on releasing your own suffering, you also hold this desire for others to have the same freedom. This is a practice you cultivate on a daily basis, not a one-time deal. It's active empathy, instead of the distancing quality of pity. When we pity someone, we distance ourselves from their experience as not being inherently like our own rather than the acceptance that we all hurt and all deserve a release from suffering.

Loving-kindness is the complement of compassion, in that you wish for the positive welfare and happiness of others. It is the opposite of conditional love.

Neither way of living requires being a pushover. You don't have to erase all your boundaries to experience these practices. You can hold compassion and loving-kindness for people without letting them hurt you. Because after all, isn't the act of hurting others separating them even further from experiencing love and a freedom from suffering?

Pema Chödrön, the Buddhist monk, talks about how hard this practice is, and how even the attempt is very healing. She suggests that in order to take this on, we start with the people we love the most in the world. Compassion and loving-kindness are easy when someone is already one of your people. Once we are fairly successful in that regard, we move into extending it to the people we aren't so sure about. The people that are a little sketchy. Finally, we move into extending it to the people who hurt us and others the most, who therefore, in reality, need this the most. The people who we aren't even sure are on Team Humanity at this point.

Holding for them the desire for true happiness and a release of suffering is the greatest gift we can give ourselves because it frees us of some of their toxicity, if not their actions themselves. It also has a powerful effect on our wellness. It releases harmful stress chemicals, it builds our immune system back up, and it activates the parts of our brain where we process empathy and emotional processing. In short, caring about the experiences of others makes us better and healthier people, so it is not as entirely selfless a practice as you may think!

Cope Onward

Even More Here-and-Now, Short-Term, Instant Gratification Coping Skills

The more coping skills you have in your back pocket, the better. If you have an array of stuff to draw from you are far less likely to fall apart. Consider it a toolbox. You may have a really fantastic screwdriver. Passed down for generations. Your grandpa used it to fix the bathtub sixty years ago. That's all well and good, except maybe it's a flat head and today is the day you need a Phillips head. My suggestion? Try any of these that sound vaguely interesting, useful, or intriguing. There is nothing wrong with having a huge, rolling cart of tools on hand at all times. And these are the types of skills that you can use in-the-moment when you are about to lose your shit. They don't require as much planning, practice, and implementation as many of the others discussed above.

1) Chew on something. Gum. Beef jerky. Pop Rocks. Something that you can focus your attention on.

2) Find something to keep your hands busy. Stuff like Play-Doh or Silly Putty are less distracting than fidget spinners, Slinkys, fidget cubes, etc. But dude, use whatever works for ya.

3) Blink. It interrupts the brain's perception of time (according to research, it may function as a way of slowing down our neural metabolism). It's essentially a system reboot/mini-nap that we do throughout our waking hours unconsciously that we can also do consciously when stressed.

4) Attach a calming scent to feeling calm, happy, and relaxed (lavender can be a good one to use since it has calming properties in

its own right). You do this by intentionally smelling a certain scent when you feel safe and relaxed. Like after meditation or guided imagery or exercising. Then carry a drop of that scent on a cotton ball in a ziplock baggie or small container. When feeling stressed, open it and inhale the scent and reconnect to the calm feeling.

5) When you find yourself thinking in negative terms of "I can'ts" (such as "I can't deal with large crowds" or "I can't run a 10K") add the word "... yet" to the end of the thought. That opens you up to the possibility of working towards being able to do it later, rather than getting stuck in a cycle of negativity.

6) Take a hot bath with Epsom salts for a detox. If you don't have access to a tub, at least soak your feet.

7) Go ahead and cry. Sad tears release chemicals that other tears do not.

8) Create a list of five things you are grateful for. Either mentally or write it down. (My mom made me do this when I was little and I hated her for it... but it so worked.)

9) Take off your shoes and socks and connect to the ground beneath you. (It's called "earthing!")

10) Hold a piece of ice in your hand. It won't actually hurt you but the sensation will disrupt the other distress signals in your body. This is an especially good coping skill if you struggle with thoughts of self-injury.

11) Count backwards from 100 by threes. Trust me, you won't be able to focus on anything but keeping those numbers organized in your mind.

12) Look at cat videos online. Or pygmy goat videos. Or panda bears. Or puppy dogs. Embrace whatever your cuteness kryptonite is for a good five minute Pomodoro break!

13) Identify whatever muscles are tense in your body and intentionally relax them one by one.

14) Visualize a stop sign in your head. And tell yourself "STOP."

15) Picture an ideal moment in your life. Put yourself back in that experience and connect to the positive feelings you associate with that time period.

16) Blow bubbles. It's damn impossible to have panic attack inducing breathing and control your breath enough to blow a bubble at the same time.

17) Get under something heavy. Weighted blankets are great, but whatever blankets you have will also do, pile them on you. Or crawl between the mattress and the box spring of your bed if that won't induce any claustrophobic feelings. As a general rule, you want a weighted blanket to be 10% of

your ideal body weight if you are an adult for maximum effect. For kiddos, it's about 10% of their current body weight plus a pound or two.

18) Sit in the sun. Vitamin D helps depression symptoms and reduces systemic inflammation in the body.

19) Gentle yoga poses (also known as forms, or by their Sanskrit word, asanas) facilitate body awareness (if the pendulation/titration exercises seem really difficult, the asanas can help move you in that direction).

20) Emotional Acupressure, known as tapping or EFT. (I wrote a zine on this, but the sequence is easy to find online and there are a ton of YouTube videos a well!)

21) Drink something warm and soothing. Coffee or tea, honey and lemon. Do caffeine-free if caffeine makes you edgy (my personal favorite comfort tea is Good Earth Sweet and

Spicy and it is available with caffeine and without).

22) Take a picture of a living thing that you love. Your boo. Your kiddo (human or fur-baby). Your bestie. A gorgeous flower. Your own damn rock-star survivor self. Take pictures of all of them. Remind yourself that there is love and beauty living out in the world.

23) Create a tiny treats budget and hit the thrift or dollar store. When I was raising my daughter on 18K a year and living off my WIC groceries, one of my favorite treat activities was to buy a dollar bottle of nail polish and give myself a pedi at home. Create a tiny fun budget for yourself. Something in the dollar to five dollar range maybe? Hit the dollar store or resale shop and treat yourself to something that's purely for fun. A bubble bath. A cheesy book. A new mug for your Sweet and Spicy tea.

24) Write a letter to someone you love or appreciate. Tell them what makes them so special to you. You can send it or not send it, but sending it might be a great boost that *they* need.

25) Write a letter to yourself. Your past self, your future self, your current self. Who could use some support and words of wisdom?

26) Take one toxic (or suspicious) thing out of your life for 21 days. A food, a substance, a shitty human being. How do you feel? Any better? What happens when you allow it (or them) back in three weeks later? Does your body say no?

27) Drink some water. Drink *a lot* of water. I don't wanna see one bit of yellow in that pee, OK? Water is as vital to the brain as it is the body. It improves our memory and our concentration. You *need* those brain cells well lubricated, am I right?

28) Reflect on something you do hella well. How'd you get so good at it? How might those skills translate to this situation?

29) Make a list of things that *don't* need to be changed in your life. What works just fucking fine?

30) Have sex, cuddle with someone, get a light touch massage, or just *think* about someone you feel close too. These are all activities that release oxytocin (deep tissue massage decreases cortisol, but light touch massage releases far more oxytocin). Oxytocin is a peptide hormone that facilitates connection and empathy. Interesting thing? While cis women are the people scientists have said have more access to (and therefore more) oxytocin (childbirth, nursing, and more likely to be relational in general), cis men are far more sensitive to oxytocin than cis women. We all need it to keep our parasympathetic nervous system online!

31) Touch not an option? Nurture relationships in other ways. Send someone a text or email thanking them or telling them how much you appreciate them. Deepening our connection with people has a stronger (positive) correlation to our health than smoking has (negative) to cancer!

32) Strike a (power) pose. Tons of research shows that when we stand like superheroes (legs apart, arms on hips, elbows bent) we feel more powerful. To the point that standing like this for two minutes decreases cortisol (the stress hormone) and increases testosterone (our engaged-to-win hormone). Channel your inner Wonder Woman or Black Panther, y'all.

33) Take a tech break (and can I just say I initially typed this as "brake" which is equally appropriate). Set up a schedule for checking your messages and social media rather than be on the obsessive constant tech check. Some people have gone so far as to grey out

their phone screens (without the bright colors to entice us, we are far more likely to fall back into the rabbit hole of mindless scrolling).

34) Picture someone or something that represents loving-kindness and compassion to you. It could be a person, a spiritual figure, or maybe an aspect of nature you resonate with. Picture yourself in the presence of this compassion and loving-kindness and feel these things towards yourself. What would you hear from it? How would these experiences feel to you?

35) Try a Tibetan singing bowl. The concentration it takes to make it hum is sort of like blowing bubbles. You have to focus so much on that, you can't focus on other stuff. (I have a friend with a neurological tremor who can focus in well enough to hold his fingers still with the bowl, and that's *amazing*. It's the only time I've seen him not shake!)

36) Do something slowly. Like, slow way down and be mindful. Or pick a task that requires

time and mindful attention (making risotto works, trust me on this one!).

37) Plan a dream trip. Is it a vacation or a learning experience? Where will you go? What will you do? Most importantly, what amazing foods will you try? Plan out all the details… you've now got an amazing goal to work toward!

38) Pick an anthem song. Play that shit when you need a pick me up. Sing along *loud*. (Mine is Sunflowers by The Velvet Janes.)

39) Smudge that shit. Seriously, the research shows that burning sage and other herbs kills toxins in the air and improves brain functions. Obvs, burning and producing smoke is better (and that's what I do at home), but at work I use a sage spray so I don't set off the smoke detectors in the building (everyone there already has enough to put up with having me around!).

40) Set your intention by saying it out loud, not just thinking it. It adds an auditory cue, making it more likely to stick.

41) Do five-seven-eight breathing. You are essentially breathing in for five counts, holding for seven, exhaling for eight. The longer exhale engages the parasympathetic response.

42) Take a break from your comfort zone. Take a different route, even if just to your mailbox. Chew your food on the other side of your mouth (you have no *idea* how weird that will feel to do intentionally if you are a creature of habit!). Pay attention to how these changes affect you, it gives you something new to focus on.

43) Make a list of things you look forward to. If the list seems small, create things to look forward to like a cupcake date with yourself at the end of the week. Anticipation produces dopamine before you even get the reward!

44) Are you really furious about something? Try the 60 minute "anger package" from Julia Samuel's book, *Grief Works*. Do 10 minutes of journaling, 20 minutes of running (or some other cardio exercise), 10 minutes of meditating, and 20 minutes of watching or reading something funny.

45) Shift your language. Say "I don't" instead of "I can't." Instead of making demands to others, state your preference to them and label it as such. These language shifts add ownership to your experience and decrease the power struggle.

46) Make one small but healthy change for 21 days and see how you feel after. Not a huge diet shift, but maybe switch out dairy milk with almond milk. Maybe do five minutes of stretching in the morning before going to work. Maybe switching to half-caff instead of fully caffeinated coffee. Something that

can have a huge impact without a ton of extra stress and planning.

47) Try a cue-controlled relaxation technique. You are just tensing and then relaxing certain muscles in your body at a time, so you can connect and feel the difference. When we are upset, we tense our muscles in certain patterns as part of our fight, flight, freeze response. By connecting back to our bodies, we can start to unpack these patterns so when they occur we know where to focus our relaxation efforts.

48) Channel your inner Dr. Phil. Step outside what's going on mentally for a moment and ask yourself, booming Texas drawl included, *"How's that workin' for ya?"* This isn't intended as a mechanism of self-shaming for whatever response you are having. Remember, responses aren't good or bad, they are all adaptive. But this does let you step out of the cycle of response for a minute

and judge if it's an adaptation that is helping you through the current situation in the healthiest way possible. So you can adjust as need be.

Helping Others Cope

Because No One in The History of Ever Has Calmed Down When Someone Told Them to Calm Down

You may have picked up this book for yourself, and only yourself. Which makes you a self-care superstar. But a lot of people pick up my books in order to support someone else who is struggling. If that's you, hopefully you found things in here that are helpful for you in the process of figuring out how to help them. I don't know anyone who couldn't benefit from some more support and tools (and if you know anyone like that, send them my way so I can study them under a microscope!).

The problem with supporting others's ability to cope is that it is so easy to fall into douchebaggery territory, by giving them the impression that they are fucked up and need to get their shit together. Even if that is an empirical truth (and chances are, as exhausting as someone is, the situation is far more complicated than that), telling them that won't get you very far.

Like, literally. Cuz they may slash your tires and then you are really stuck.

A question I get a lot is: how do you approach supporting someone without enabling bad behavior or taking away their autonomy by insisting they do things exactly your way? No one wants to go into one of these conversations being an asshole, but we've all said things the wrong way at some point.

So here are some ideas for lessening the likelihood of a cope-er-vention fail.

- Honor their experience and emotional response. Anything we feel is valid and real.

- Recognize that no one goes from 0 to 100 instantaneously. They were probably already at 99. They may be good at hiding the fact, or you may have missed the signs, but if it seems like they flipped out at something small, it likely was a proverbial last straw piled on top of everything else they have been trying to manage.

- Without saying you understand exactly how they feel (because no one knows *exactly*, right?) discuss your own experiences with coping with tough times. Talk about who and what helped you the most. Talk about where you maybe had to recognize that your very real feelings weren't always representative of reality due to your own emotional history and how you shifted your thinking. Elicit hope for the future.

- Give them this book. Show them that *dude*, this is a normal physiological response and they are being badass humans dealing with an exhausted system.

- Help them figure out behavioral chunks they can tackle with your help that don't feel overwhelming. Maybe you can go over and help them clean up the kitchen. Maybe you can go hiking together. If it is an activity that will benefit the both of you that's more the better, right?

- Remind them that you only want to help, if your help is truly beneficial. Don't do unwanted things. Don't make them feel like they have to assign you a task to make you feel useful. Tell them directly "I do not need to help you to make myself feel better, I want to help you if it will actually help you."

- If they say they don't want help and support, leave the door open for later support. Tell them if anything changes you are available to help and would genuinely like to.

- Get trained in suicide prevention if you haven't already. Be brave in asking those difficult questions. A good training that is all online and will only take an hour of your time can be found here: tinyurl.com/ASKCertificationTraining

Remember that someone may be in a bad place, and their response to their experiences can end up directed toward you. Or toward people you love or care for (like your kids, for example). And hey, you can understand where someone is coming from but not allow bad behavior. Establish boundaries and communicate the consequences of them not being respected. Follow through on the consequences. If contact becomes limited because of these behaviors, communicate what new behaviors you need to see before contact is reestablished.

An Empowering Conclusion Before You Face the World Yet Again

This book was originally a tiny zine. It contained basic coping skill ideas that had come from my practice as a therapist and as a human being with my own problems to deal with. And since I am not the only person in the world who needs to use coping skills on the regular, I asked others what worked for them and saw several common themes that informed my original ideas.

The idea was to remind us of what works. And to offer other possible tools when your toolbox has become depleted.

Even though the zine was tiny, it wasn't conceptually basic. So many readers shared that they experienced shifts in their thinking and their relationship with themselves over the ideas that were in it. In a world in crisis, we are all so deeply hungry for some real fucking talk about self-care and how that is the foundation that propels us toward systemic change.

Expanding the original zine into this book took me some time because I wanted that same message to hold true.

We aren't talking about coping skills as merely taking hot baths and breathing better, but of holding onto our own sense of self-value even if we are the only ones doing so. There is no political strategy more radical than that. There is nothing else you can do in the world to cause a seismic shift larger than that.

I asked people to tell me not what their coping skills were so much, but what their relationship with their coping skills had become as they practiced active strategies. That was probably a pretty confusing question, but two people totally got what I was saying (probably because both had been interns of mine in the past?) and sent me the following responses:

I remember my entire world changed when I heard Don Jose Ruiz ask: When you pray, who do you think is listening?

That's when I realized that everything I ever needed was already inside of me and I had the power to let go or to make things happen. The power of me became evident when I realized I was always the one fulfilling my own prayers through actions or thoughts. Not sure if this makes sense but it was life changing for me. Now I don't have to rely on things outside of me to make me feel OK because I've always been the one. –Melody Montano

The biggest thing I have learned in my journey is that you teach people how to treat you. It is my responsibility to set and reinforce my boundaries and to ask for what I need. Nobody can read my mind and it is not their job to. Honestly, when I started to actually apply this, it changed my life. I can now own my shit and take responsibility for it instead of avoiding it or blaming someone else for it. I'm constantly checking in with myself when I feel unhappy or stuck. I ask myself what do I need and how do I get it and call myself out when I'm being ridiculous. Even when it sucks to do so. –Lisa Arce

I've known both of these people for some years now. I promise that their lives have not been easy, and neither are trying to over-simplify the complexities of a toxic world. They are saying that fighting for self-empowerment and self-control and self-responsibility is what carried them through, when they weren't getting what they needed from others.

In a system designed to break us, choose to no longer be broken.

References

Achor, Shawn. *The Happiness Advantage: The Seven Principles that Fuel Success and Performance at Work*. Virgin, 2011.

"Autonomic nervous system." *Autonomic nervous system - an overview | ScienceDirect Topics*, www.sciencedirect.com/topics/neuroscience/autonomic-nervous-system.

Center For Deployment of Psychology. "Cognitive Behavior Therapy For Depression." 15 Mar. 2018.

Chodron, Pema. *Places That Scare You: A Guide to Fearlessness in Difficult Times*. Shambhala, 2018.

Cirillo, Francesco. *The Pomodoro Technique: Do More and Have Fun with Time Management*. FC Garage, 2013.

"Create Joy and Satisfaction." *Mental Health America*, 4 Feb. 2014, www.mentalhealthamerica.net/create-joy-and-satisfaction.

Damasio, Antonio R. *Looking for Spinoza: joy, sorrow, and the feeling brain*. Harcourt, 2003.

"Do men and women release the same amounts of oxytocin when they are in love?" *Quora*, www.quora.com/Do-men-and-women-release-the-same-amounts-of-oxytocin-when-they-are-in-love.

Draeger, Lars. *Navy SEAL training guide: mental toughness*. Special Operations Media, 2013.

Dupin, Lucile, et al. "Generalized movement representation in haptic perception." *Journal of Experimental Psychology: Human Perception and Performance*, vol. 43, no. 3, 2017, pp. 581–595., doi:10.1037/xhp0000327.

Freud, Anna. (1937). *The Ego and the Mechanisms of Defense*, London: Hogarth Press and Institute of Psycho-Analysis.

Freud, Sigmund. (1894). *The Neuro-psychoses of Defence*. SE, 3: 41-61.

Freud, Sigmund. (1896). *Further Remarks on the Neuro-psychoses of Defence*. SE, 3: 157-185.

Ganim, Barbara, and Fox, Susan. *Visual Journaling: Going Deeper than Words*. Quest Books, Theosophical Pub. House, 1999.

Gowin, Joshua. "Why Your Brain Needs Water." *Psychology Today*, Sussex Publishers, 15 Oct. 2010, www.psychologytoday.com/blog/you-illuminated/201010/why-your-brain-needs-water

Korba, Rodney J. "The Rate of Inner Speech." *Perceptual and Motor Skills*, vol. 71, no. 3, 1990, pp. 1043–1052., doi:10.2466/pms.1990.71.3.1043.

Harper, F. (2010). Walking the Good Red Road: Storytelling in the Counseling Relationship Using the Film Dreamkeeper. *Journal of Creativity in Mental Health, 5*(2), 216-220. doi:0.1080/15401383.2010.485119

Hofmann, Stefan G., et al. *Clinical psychology review*, U.S. National Library of Medicine, Nov. 2011, www.ncbi.nlm.nih.gov/pmc/articles/PMC3176989/.

Hollis, James. *Living an examined life: wisdom for the second half of the journey*. Sounds True, Inc., 2018.

Jordan, Judith V. *Relational-Cultural therapy*. American Psychological Association, 2018

Lamott, Anne. *Plan B: further thoughts on faith*. Riverhead Books, 2006.

Lazarus, Richard S., Folkman, Susan (1984). *Stress, appraisal, and coping*. Springer.

Levine, Peter A. *Waking the tiger: healing trauma*. North Atlantic Books, 1997.

Mohagheghzadeh, Abdolali, et al. "Medicinal smokes." *Journal of Ethnopharmacology*, vol. 108, no. 2, 2006, pp. 161–184., doi:10.1016/j.jep.2006.09.005.

Moonshine, Cathy. *Acquiring competency and achieving proficiency with dialectical behavior therapy*. PESI, 2008.

Moore, Kellie B. "Does Oxytocin Give Women an Edge? It's Not Quite That Simple." *Verily*, 16 May 2016, verilymag.com/2016/05/oxytocin-sex-differences-women-hormones-bonding-sex-trust.

Najavits, Lisa M. *Seeking safety: a treatment manual for PTSD and substance abuse*. The Guilford Press, 2003.

Ober, Clinton, et al. *Earthing: the most important health discovery ever?* Read How You Want, 2014.

Pappas, Stephanie. "Oxytocin: Facts About the Cuddle Hormone." *LiveScience*, Purch, 4 June 2015, www.livescience.com/42198-what-is-oxytocin.html.

"Pendulation, trauma release and bodywork." *First of Nine: Tensegrity Blog*, 21 Aug. 2013, firstofnine.wordpress.com/2011/11/13/pendulation-trauma-release-and-bodywork/.

Porges, Stephen W. *The polyvagal theory: neurophysiological foundations of emotions, attachment, communication, and self-Regulation*. W.W. Norton, 2011.

Rosenb, Robin S. "Why You May Want to Stand Like a Superhero." *Psychology Today*, Sussex Publishers, 14 July 2011, PsychologyToday.com/blog/the-superheroes/201107/why-you-may-want-stand-superhero

Samuel, Julia. *Grief works: stories of life, death and surviving*. Doubleday Canada, 2018.

"Vitamin D and depression." *Vitamin D Council*, www.vitamindcouncil.org/health-conditions/depression/.

Weiten, Wayne, et al. *Psychology applied to modern life: adjustment in the 21st century*. Cengage Learning, 2018.

"Why Do We Cry? The Science of Crying." *Time*, Time, time.com/4254089/science-crying/.

Zimmermann, Kim Ann. "Memory Definition & Types of Memory." *LiveScience*, Purch, 27 Feb. 2014, www.livescience.com/43713-memory.html.

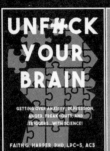

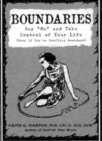